GW00703313

The Tree

Don French

 en Press

First published in Great Britain by Pen Press

All paper used in the printing of this book has been made from
wood grown in managed, sustainable forests.

ISBN13: 978-1-907499-03-6

Printed and bound in the UK
Pen Press is an imprint of Indepenpress Publishing Limited
25 Eastern Place
Brighton
BN2 1GJ

A catalogue record of this book is available from
the British Library

Cover design by Jacqueline Abromeit

*To the love of my life, my late wife Joy
who inspired this work and gave my life meaning*

About the Author

I am Don French, a retired Local Government Officer.

One of six children I was born in 1931 and lived in Hayes, Middlesex. Because of the lack of air raid shelters my schooling was limited to two days a week and even then I spent more time in air raid shelters reading comic books than learning.

At nine years old I was diagnosed as suffering from St. Vitas Dance and sent to a nursing home (that was run by nuns) in Essex. I have always had a desire to write and have started telling of the time I spent there in a story I call 'Dancing with a Saint'.

I left school at fourteen with very little education and in spite of being dyslexic, fulfilled my childhood ambition and became an Electrician. In the seventies I was appointed as an Electrical Craft Instructor by 'The London Borough of Hillingdon's Apprentices Training Scheme'. After that they employed me as a Building Services Electrical/Mechanical Officer.

I took early retirement shortly after my wife Joy, who I married in 1958, died.

When my wife Joy, the love of my life, died, I wrote a poem – *There Was A Time* and have been, when the mood takes me, writing poetry since.

Contents

BEHIND MY EYES

Come with me to a place no man has been before.
There I will show you so many things, some frightening,
some funny, others sad.

You will see things that are tragic, funny, common and rare,
nondescript or awe-inspiring.

You will not have to travel far, for all these things are as
close to you as I am, but the space between us could span a
thousand years.

Come and join me in the depth of my mind,
Delve deep into my soul.
Absorb my thoughts.
Live my dreams.
Feel my joy and my sorrow.

Come, come, come.
And join me.
Behind my eyes.

THE TREE

The tree it stood so tall and proud, that mighty, mighty oak
And when they said it must come down
We thought it was no joke.

That tree had stood so tall and proud
for nigh three hundred years
And when old Sam, he heard the news
Well, he broke down in tears.

Poor Sam he was the village fool
Not that was always so
But when he lost his darling wife
His senses all sank low.

Poor Sam, the only life he lived
Was all inside his head
His mind was blank, his eyes were glazed
Just like the living dead.

Underneath that old oak tree
Old Sam would sit and linger
Dreaming of his wedding day
And his darling, darling Lynda.

Summer, winter, autumn, spring
Sam sat beneath that oak
Dreaming of long, long ago
When life was 'Okay Doke.'

That mighty oak had started life

When Sam's ancestors were born
Now like Sam it was so old
An object of the young's scorn.

The tree will really have to go
The developers declared
That shocked old Sam back into life
And down the road he hared.

He came back with a shotgun
And leaned against the tree
With eyes ablaze he told the men
'You'll have to cut down me!'

"You'll soon move," the axe man said
A chain saw he held steady
But he froze as old Sam's gun
Was pointing at the ready.

"This tree has stood three hundred years,"
Said Sam, "It's older than the town
"So don't you try to harm it,
Or I will gun you down."

As he leaned against the tree
Old Sam could feel its life
As did long, long ago
When he first kissed his wife.

On that day long, long ago
As they sat in its cool shade
And kissed beneath that old, old Oak
A life long vow was made.

They vowed their love would last
For all their life and longer

And like the oak that grew so strong
Their love, it grew much stronger.

"Don't be a fool, put down the gun,"
The chief policeman said.
With tear-stained eyes, Sam replied
"Not until you shoot me dead."

"Come now Sam, the tree's so old
It's useful life is done,
"Come now Sam," the chiefman coaxed
"Please put down your gun."

The gun stayed firmly in his hands
For old Sam could clearly see
What a crime they would commit
If those men cut down that tree.

The branches of the tree did creak
A noise came from its bark
As old Sam watched the sun go down
And the world grow grey and dark.

Summer passed and autumn too
Then winter cruelly came
And still Sam sat beneath that tree
And the world now knew his name.

"God bless you Sam," the banners read
As campfires cheerfully glowed
And people came from far and near
Along the village road.

They kept him warm and fed him well
As people came in droves to see
The local village idiot

Give his life up for a tree.

Of all the gifts that Sam received
The clothes, the food, the claret
The one he loved best of all
Was a multi-coloured parrot.

"The Rule of Law must be enforced."
A learned Judge pronounced.
"Not while I can lift my gun!"
Our hero Sam announced.

"SAM TO BE ARRESTED."
The banner headlines read.
"Not while we're still here!"
The tree protesters said.

The village was packed, the pubs were full
And freely flowed the beer.
The tree was proudly standing still
In Sam's protest, second year.

"Send in the troops" the word went out
"We must win at any cost!"
And a sadness came about the camp
Was the battle...Lost?

The tanks rolled in that morning
They flattened all the camp
And only poor old Sam was left
As the summer Sun
It sank.

Their hulking great big leader
Demanded of our Sam;
"Get up! Get up! Get up from there!

You silly little man."

When old Sam refused to move
He grabbed him by the throat
And as he did his eyes grew large
And a scream came from his throat.

"The tree's alive!" the chief-man yelled
Running at the double
"It said we must leave Sam alone
Or we'll be in real trouble."

When their leader turned and fled
His men they did the same
When the protesters saw them go
They all came back again.

"Why did they go? Why did they flee?"
Someone slurped upon some claret
"Don't ask me," old Sam he said
"You'd better ask the Parrot."

It's three years now, the tree's still there
And so is dear old Sam.
The people come from far and near
By car, by bus, by pram.

For the children love old silly Sam
And they love his tree
I know that this is oh so true.
Silly Sam
That's me!

MY POEMS

I have written lots of poems, most of them in rhyme
If no one ever reads them
What a waste of time!

Some of them are funny, some of them are crude
Some are really filthy, others mildly rude.

One starts off romantic, but it's really not
It's all about a woman who can't control her snot.
Another one's about a boy who has made an art
Of the noises he can make, when he lets out a fart.

I wrote one about a Drum Major who was beaten in a race
By a drummer and a bugler, and where they stuck his mace.
Another tells the story of how nasty things accrue
And what a nasty trick it is, to put cling film on the loo.

There is one about some smelly feet, it really is quite sad
It tells how a bloke got married to a wife he's never had.
There is one about a Marshal, who don't do very much
Since a whore called Sexy Lill shot him in the crotch.

There is one about old silly Sam
Who tried to protect a mighty oak
Told the world it had a heart
And proved it when it spoke.

I could go on and on about what I've wrote in rhyme
But if you read them for yourself
I know you'll know they're mine!

A WAR OUT THERE

I am living like a hermit and acting like a fool, in this land
of freedom where the violent rule.

There is of course a war out there, that is plain for all to see,
and I wonder if there will ever be, peace for the likes of me.

There is of course a war out there, and I want to cry, for I'm
afraid of living and I'm afraid to die.

Once I was young and I was strong, in this land where I
belong.
Now I am old, and feeble too, my face is pale my hands are
blue.

I live in fear, and wonder why I am so afraid to die.

I'd love to walk the streets at night, or sit out in the park,
but the likes of me can never go out after dark.

There is of course a war out there, but you wouldn't know if
you listen to the politicians on the radio.

They say that all is well in this land of liberty and I wonder
why they are so blind and why they will not see the things
that worry me.

There is, hate, greed and violence out there in the street and
I don't think that I'll find peace until my God I meet.

The 'Planers' built a haven of steel and concrete and herded

us like animals to keep us off the street.
There are, no trees there is no park. There is fear and
loneliness after dark.

None venture on the street at night, unless they are looking
for a fight.

There is no light of day ever in my home. I 'm so scared and
lonely. It is hell to live alone!

Now muggers do their work by day, children in the Park
can't play.

There is violence in the air out there. The young and old are
in despair.

There is a war out there you see! No peace, no hope for the
likes of me.

Behind bolted doors and windows barred I gaze out on the
concrete yard.

It's drab and bare no sign of trees, nothing for my eyes to
please.

And as I look I wonder why, I am so afraid to die.

DUCKS

They were throwing stones at ducks they were ,when they
were firmly told:
"Stop that here and now," by a woman who was old.
Angry at the woman who had tried to spoil their fun,
one said:
"Let's tip her wheelchair up!" and that deed was done
They laughed to see that woman lying upside down
Then decided it would be fun to really go to town.

They prodded her with fingers, and tugged hard at her hair
Then lifted up her skirt and had a look down there.
They were laughing fit to kill almost having fits
When one of them suggested, "Let's get out her tits!"

She was sobbing fit to die, praying in despair
When one of them went flying, flying through the air.
He landed in the duck pond, thrown there by a bloke
Who thought that their abusing her was beyond a joke.

The others furious at what that bloke had done
Set out to attack him and landed one by one
Thrown into the duck pond by the bloke
Who had spoiled their fun.

Soaking wet and stinking, covered in green slime
They thought was punishment enough for their petty crime.
But the bloke he thought different...
and forced them on their hands and knees

To crawl around the town, with their trousers down.

Each one had a placard covering their bum
With words that told the jeering crowds
Exactly what they had done.
To that woman in her chair
So to the police he did declare.

"The punishment was fitting for what those scum bags done
To that poor old Woman who could have been my Mum.
"The law's the Law", he was told and now he understands
The police are the enforcers he can't take it into his hands.

Now he must spend three years in prison
And those boys don't give two fucks
They are having too much fun
Beating up old ladies and killing loads of ducks!

CORNER CAFÉ

A man walked in a corner side café
And for a chocolate pudding he did pay
The waitress took his money
Then brought him one with honey

And everybody in there heard him say:

"That's not my pudding!
I ordered chocolate!"

The waitress who really was sincere
Whispered very softly in his ear
"Mister be a good'un and eat this honey puddin'
'Cause we have no chocolate puddin' on today."

She dropped the honey puddin' on the floor
As from his mouth there came a mighty roar.

"I paid for chocolate!
For a chocolate pudding I did pay
So go and fetch one right away
And when you bring my puddin'
It had better be a good'un
Or I'm telling you there will be...
hell to pay!"

A man walked from a corner side café
All covered in treacle!
'Cause they had no chocolate pudding on that day.

SINGING IN THE RAIN

My mind was in a torment. My life was in a mess.
I'd been alone since God knows when.
I was depressed, I guess.

I was so sad and lonely, living without love.
A woman needs a man in life.
To hold, to kiss, to hug.

It was a stormy sultry night when I went out to complain
To a fellow who was singing
Singing in the rain.

"I'm singing in the rain," he said, "Though I don't have a
bob.
And I don't know where I'll get one, 'cause I haven't got a
job.
But it's a lovely night out here. The stars shine bright above.
It's a lovely night my dear. A night just made...for love.

To love the things that nature gives to fill us with delight.
Moonbeams dancing on the trees are such a lovely sight.
With no ties to hold me down my dear I can clearly see
The glory of creation dear
Come and sing with me!

A sadder man than me my dear would be hard to find
Until I started singing to ease my troubled mind.
Come and sing with me my dear. Let's dance out in the rain,
and free that troubled mind of yours from the humdrum
pain."

I joined him singing in the rain, beneath the stars above.
We sang and danced throughout that night.
A night just made for love.

I felt at one with nature. My troubles fell away.
We danced and sang and kissed and loved until the break of
day.

As the sun shone on the rooftops and the birds began to
sing,
He said; "Last night I was a pauper. Today I am a King!"

I told my friend about last night. And oh! How she did
beam;
"It did not rain last night," She said
"You just had a wet dream!"

I'm in my early fifties, I cope the best I can,
But frustration can play funny tricks.
On a lass without a man.

Yet if it was a dream I had, then only heaven knows
Why my shoes are soaking wet, so too my outdoor clothes.

BAG LADY

Oh! I felt so sad, for that lady with her bag,
as she trudged along the street the other day.
Her clothes were old and torn.
Her shoes were scuffed and worn,
and her hair was oh so dull and oh so grey.
Everything she had was contained inside a bag,
that someone better off had thrown away.

When like a poor lost child she looked at me and smiled,
I didn't know what to do or what to say,
so I simply turned my head and walked away.

Later I did find she was dwelling on my mind,
'cause I wondered how she ever got that way
Did she ever have a lover?
Was she a wife, was she a mother?

Perhaps I should find out, some other day!

Last night after dark I found her in the park,
she had laid down on a bench and passed away.
Now I wish I'd helped her out that other day,
but just to prove I care I washed her face and hair,
and her frowns and worried lines all smoothed away.

So she looked her very best,
as I laid her out to rest,
but I wonder if she would have,
died that way if I'd had,
helped her out the other day.

ANNIE

My girlfriend's mother at the age of, sixty three
Got very drunk, one night and got in bed with me.
(She said)
I haven't had none since nineteen eighty-two,
and that's why sunshine, I'm here in bed
Bed with you.

So when I saw the hunger
the hunger, in her eyes,
for my girlfriend's mother,
I thought I should oblige.
So I did!

My girlfriend's grandma, at the age of sixty-three
Saw me in the bath one day
and got in there with me.

She said;
I've haven't had none,
since nineteen eighty-two.
And from what my daughter
tells me, it's very nice with you.

So when I saw the hunger
the hunger, in her eyes,
for my girlfriend's grandma,
I thought, I must oblige.

Then my girlfriend Annie,
at the age of twenty-one,

found out what to her gran,
and mum I'd done.

All the blooming three of them,
at me they laugh and scoff.
Because I'm no good to none of them
Annie broke it off!

BEN'S HAT

I suppose you think I look a proper prat,
wearing this old peculiar hat.

But I paid my last penny, on this hat I call my Benny,
'cause you got to wear a hat to ride a bike.

I suppose you think I look a proper sight, riding in me
Benny on me bike.

But, I am not so silly, there's a helmet on my willy and it's
for the bike I'm going to ride tonight.

COUNTRY COTTAGE

Ever since the day that I was born
I've heard the blast of the blooming car horn.

Engines roaring
The ringing of phones
Aircraft noises that rattle my bones
I'll tell you friend it gets me down
Living here in this crap town.

A cottage in the country, that's where I'd like to be.
Fishing in a duck pond, or climbing up a tree.

Feeding corn to chickens. Chopping up some logs.
Stroking at an old goats beard. Or romping with some dogs.

Strolling through a meadow. Roaming in a wood.
Breathing in some pure clean air. Wouldn't that be good?

But, I don't live in the country. I live in a town.
Where people never wear a smile. Because living gets them
down.

With cars horns always honking. Planes droning in the sky.
Drug crazed scumbags mugging. It's no wonder why.
A cottage in the country is where I want to be.
Fishing in the old duck pond, or sitting in a tree."

BOTTOM LINERS

Poor old Pat has lost her hat
And she is broken hearted.
Poor old Pat she lost her hat
It blew off when she farted.

***

Oysters are plentiful , and shrimps are too,
But here's some advice I give to you.
Winkles are very hard to find, I've found,
When you've put your trousers on
The wrong way around!

***

I didn't know whether to cry or laugh
At what I saw upon my path.
My neighbours thought it was good fun
To see what their Great Dane had done.

***

Well! I've seen a cow, and I've seen a pig!
But I've never! Ever seen, a turd, that big!

***

There is no woman in my life.
I'm right out of luck.
The only bird I've stuffed this year.
Is the Christmas duck.

FRIAR TUCK

"There's many a woman that I have rode!", bragged old
Friar Tuck
"There's many a woman that I have rode, and many a more
I'll truck!

There's many a woman that I have known who can't resist
the need!
To dive upon this Holy Man and ride him like a steed!

Yeah! There's many a woman that I have know who's
ha'penny they will part
For a ride upon this Friar's back when there's no room
inside my cart!"

THE WIFE'S STORY

It's a long lonely road I must travel.
It's a long lonely hill that I climb.
For I am in love with two people
and neither of them can be mine.

Fate has treated me cruelly
it robbed true love from my life.
I know my husband adores me, but can't treat me like a
wife.

He broke his back in a car crash and in a wheelchair must
live.
Now all the love that I have for him, to another I give.

We meet each week on a Wednesday, for a night of
passionate deeds
I know this other man loves me and he fulfils all my needs.

If I was free we could marry but that can never be
For I will not leave my husband, no matter how crippled he
be.

Yes I'm in love with two people and I know they both love
me.
One is chained to a wheelchair, for the other one day a week
I am free.

DECEIT

Life is a long lonely road, I must travel
It's a steep stony hill that I climb.
For I'm in love with a woman
Who I know just will never be mine.

Her smile is the smile of an angel.
Her kisses much sweeter than wine.
But, she is wed to another
So I know she'll just never be mine!

I should go away and forget her
And find a new love of my own.
But I sit patiently waiting
Knowing tonight she will phone.

She will call and tell me she needs me
And in warm arms I will sleep.
And then I will travel my long lonely road
Until she calls me again next week!

Then her smile will be one of an angel.
Her kisses much sweeter than wine.
And for a short while I'll be happy to know
That for one night a week
She's just mine.

THE EYE OF THE CANE

There was a man, a sad, sad man
Old before his time
Who walked head down dejectedly
Come rain, come snow, come shine.

He trudged dejected through the streets
A sadness in his eye
The man had lost all zest for life
He just lived to die.

He walked into a charity shop
To shelter from the rain,
His eyes fell on a walking stick
A silver orb topped cane.

A cane of shiny ebony
On its orb, an etched closed eye
That opened up and winked at him
As the man walked by.

Coming from that charity shop
He held the cane with pride
Walking with great dignity
And a long and easy stride.

He walks the street with head held high
And smiles at passers-by, holding a cane of ebony
with it's closed yet seeing eye.

It sees much sadness in the world

And it likes to try,
To give back pride and dignity
To those who want to die.

It chooses some to do it's work
That closed yet seeing eye
To prove to them that life is good
And show the reason why.

A friendly smile, a kindly nod
Will lighten up the day
For those who think
There is no time in life
To smile or to play.

That cane with its closed seeing eye
Creates the same sensation
As it did long, long ago
In the hand of a long, long dead
Free Mason.

THOUGHTS

Will the thoughts with in my head
Disappear when I am dead?
Will the stars up in the sky
Fade away when I die?
Will the things I think and feel
Come to nothing...Be unreal?
Will they all die when I'm dead
Or just stay trapped within my head?
Will I fly up to the stars or
Collapse like a house of cards?
Is there a God, an afterlife
Will I join my darling wife?
Did Jesus die upon a cross?
Will my heart and soul be lost?
Is the voice inside my head
My darling wife, who is long dead?
Is there nothing left of her
For my grieving heart to stir?
If there is no afterlife
Why do I still hear my wife?
Why do I still feel her near?
And why do I no longer fear?
The fear of dying will have no qualms
If I'm in my loved one's arms.
If there is no God above ,there's always hope
There's always love
Because the love she gave to me will last for all eternity.

DRUM MAJOR

I'm a sophisticated singer, of sophisticated songs
I sing of little birds, and I sing of dings and dongs
I don't sing of cuddly bears like Paddington or Mogley
But I sing about a woman with a multi coloured boggy

The song I'm gonna sing now is going to be me last
It's all about a fellow with a mace stuck up his...
Da Da Da Da. DA da da da. Da Da.

The Queen was coming to visit. Arrangements had been
made
For a big brass band to lead a big parade.
In the music room they were having fun
The bugler with his bugle. And the drummer with his drum.

BOOM...BOOM...BOOM...BOOM
    BAA, BAA, BAA.
    ...BER...BAA!

The Drum Major was a sobbing as he got into his gear
His poor old head was throbbing 'cause he'd been on the
beer
And when your head is throbbing it's not a lot of fun
To hear a bugler bugle and a drummer bang a drum.

    BANG... BANG.... BANG... BANG
      BANG...BANG.
    BOOM...BER...BAA!

But he must lead the band out, or there would be a riot

So he devised a plan, to keep the whole thing quiet!
The drumsticks and the bugle he hid in the drummer's drum
And stuffed the trombones with some socks just to make them hum.

He used some cotton wool to mute the flute
And inside of the trumpet he wedged a hobnail boot!

> DA...DA...DA...DA
> DA DA DA
> DA...DAA!

The Drum Major lead the band out with a smile upon his face
As he marched along so proudly twiddling with his mace.

"Where is the buglers bugle?" The Prince was heard to shout.
"And someone tell the drummer to give his drum a clout!"
"But where are the drummers drumsticks?" The Queen was heard to ask.
"They are with the buglers...bugle!" Said the Major as he past.

The cornet player gave a yell and firmly hit the deck
As the boot flew from the trumpet and smacked him in the neck.

Over his prone body four trombonist fell, and the drummer
And the bugler. And a bloke that played a bell.

On marched the proud Drum Major oblivious to the fuss
He was twiddling with his mace and never saw the bus,

The bus was full of tourist visiting the town!
It swerved to miss the Major and knocked the grandstand down.

DA...DA...DA...DA
DA, DA, DA,
DA...DAA!

The bugler blew his bugle and the drummer banged his drum
And after the Drum Major the whole brass band did run.
Back came the sad Drum Major, on his face a look of fear!
A drumstick in each earhole and a mace stuck up his rear!

DA...DA...DA...DA
DA,DA,DA
DA, DAA!

That's why that old Drum Major
Will always wear a frown!
When ever it is mentioned
That 'The Queen' may come to
TOWN!

MAD FOR LOVE

I was going mad for love, when I met a woman in a pub
She was built just like a tub, a great big tub of lard.
I told her that I fancied her.

She said,"I'm very flattered sir,
but you're not the kind that I prefer.
You are far too old
And ugly."

Well! I thought that comment was absurd, coming from that
sad old bird, who had a nose shaped like a turd
All knobbly and crust-rated

So I finished up my pint of beer, growled at her "Good night
my dear." And went off home frustrated.

SENTIMENTAL CLAPTRAP

I don't want your sentimental claptrap.
I don't want your lovey dove advice.

Don't want your sentimental claptrap!
You have made your bed, you pay the price.
You come here and say you really, really love me
And that we are fools to stay apart.
But I recall the day when you went away
And left me with a broken bleeding heart.

So don't give me your sentimental claptrap
Don't tell me you're crying every day.
'Cause you silly little flirt, if you dish the dirt
That is just the price you have to pay.
You come here and say you really love me
But your voice is full of if's and but's.
So you can take your sentimental claptrap
And stick it where the monkey
Sticks its...NUTS!

DOOR BELL SONG

My door bell's very high, and hers is very low, which causes
us a problem when a courting we do go,
because she is very short and I am very long
I can't ding her ding a ding, ding,
and she can't dang my dong!

So we get no ding a ding, ding, no ding, ding, ding! No ding
a ding ding, dang dong!

One day she said to me, 'Us two could be in clover, if we
could find a handy man to change our door bells over.'
Well! We paid a bloke to do it, but the bloke he did it
wrong. 'Cause now I've got her ding a ding, ding, and she
has got my dong!

Yeah, the bloke we paid to do it was a silly mush
because when he changed the door bells he didn't change
the push!

One day I said to her, "We will soon be courting proper!"
And I went down the hardware shop, and bought myself
a knocker!

Now we are getting married soon and she is looking swell!
Because since she's used my knocker, we have rung
the bell!

PYGMY MAN

Here's the story of a pygmy man,
who got married to an Amazon.

Where she was large he was so small ,
that they had no loving at all.

One day while on the village green
the whole world heard that Pygmy scream:

Oh! Oh! Oh! I...!
Got a pain in my...DONG !
'Cause my Dong! Is to long to fit in its throng!

We could never relate,
while my dong was size six and her ding is size eight
So she put a wasp in my throng,
and a wasp don't belong in side a chap's throng!

But I have planned my revenge!
Yes I'll get my revenge
Just as soon as she bends.

Then tears to her eyes I willl bring, when I stick this wasp
right up her DING!

TONE DEAF

I'm tone deaf, I've got no rhythm, I hope for that I'll be
forgiven, because:

> I'm as silly as ear holes!
> I'm as daft as can be.
> I'm as silly as ear holes!
> There's no one as silly as me.

I can't play a tune on a trumpet,
on the old piano can't thump it,
I can't strum one on a guitar,
but I could be a great big super star.
Because:

> I can play a tune on my Do! Da!
> Yes
> I can play a tune on my Do! Da!

And I could be a great big super star. If I knew were to go.
If I knew who to show my...DO!..DA!

I suppose I really shouldn't have oughta, but I showed the
bloke next door and his daughter.
They thought it was good fun,
but I won't tell you what they have done
with my Do! Do Do Do! Da!...
Ahhhhhhhhhhhhh!

BULL

I was young, I was young, I was young, and so strong!
I'd walk the town, just singing this song!

I'm a bull, I'm a bull, I'm a bull of a man!
I will make love to whoever I can!
Be it Peggy, or Doreen, or Shirley, or Ann!
I'm a Bull ... I'm a Bull ... Of a Man! ... So I am!

Now I'm old, yes I'm old, I can't do what I did.
Where I once was a man, now I'm more like a squid!
So bring in a coffin! And nail down the lid!
On this poor old wreck of a man!
Poor old chap.

SEX GOD

I'm a sex God! A sex God. A sex God I am!
I'll take a woman whenever I can.

Married or single, I don't give a damn!
A sex God! A sex God. A sex God I am!

I fancy all women, that's plain to see.
But I've never yet found one.
Who fancies me.

SNOT

I was feeling so romantic.
I was ready to propose.
When a snort came from her snozzel.
And a bogey from her nose.

It was the biggest bogey
That I have ever seen.
Some of it was yellow
The rest of it was green.

She looked at me and smiled
And I had to grin
As that muti-coloured bogey
Dangled from her chin.

It formed into a bubble
And as her lips she pursed
The bubble grew much bigger.
And then that bubble burst.

That bubble busted bogey
Was yellow, green and black.
And with her little finger
She stuffed that bogey back.

Well! Now my story's over
I never did propose.
I won't wed no woman
With that lot up her nose.

DUNG BEETLE

Long ago there lived a king, who died very young.
He was buried in a tomb, and sad, sad songs were sung.
The pyramids along The Nile, that glisten in the sun.
Were all inspired by that boy king, and a beetle that rolls dung!

Dung beetles do not have no fun, they have no fun at all
They spend their entire lives rolling up a big dung ball.
They lay an egg inside the ball, and by its side will wait
For the egg that they have laid to slowly incubate.

And when the egg begins to hatch, and they hear their baby cry
They lay down contented, and slowly fade and die.
Inside the ball a grub does munch and munch and munch and munch
At the ball that they had made for its dinner, tea and lunch.

It eats so much and grows so fat it falls into a stupor.
It grows so fat it bursts its skin and turns into a pupa.
For weeks and weeks it lays like dead
Them from that pupa pops a head.

That pupas head is strong and black
And at the dung ball it does whack
The newborn beetles heard the call
It must get out and roll a ball.

It must get out and roll in dung
A beetle's work is never done.

A dung beetle
And ancient king
Were the inspiration
For the pyramids along The Nile,
And belief in reincarnation!

NO MORE CURRY FOR YOU MY SON

I'll tell you this I will my son.
You are not the only one,
The only one to ever have
An accident outside the Lav.
I know you tried your best to bake it.
But you almost knew you'd never make it.

I saw you in a frantic hurry
Driven by a red hot curry
You barely made it to the door
Arse on fire and all sore.

"The door is locked!" You did complain.
But erupted just the same.

Now you claim it's your intent
To find a commode you can rent.
Because you feel that will prevent
Another curry, accident.

SLOB!

My wife said how I behave will send me to an early grave
For to go a week without a shave really is disgusting.
I told her to shut her gob because, I know! I am a slob.
                    YES!
I'm a slob box. I'm a slob box, a slob box I am!
I've got ears full of wax, and toes full of jam!
I've got snot up my nose, and fluff in me belly!
And my feet do stink 'cause I've peed in me welly.

FARM YARD

If you come down to our farm
You are in for a surprise.
There is something going on down there.
You wont believe your eyes.

Birds have gathered in the trees
And are singing songs for us
The sheep the ducks the cows and geese
All join in the chorus.

But the donkey and the pony
Well, they don't sing of course
Because the donkey and the pony
Are both a little ...Horse.

The monkey has a tail
A tale to relate
About a hippopotamus.
Who was looking for a mate.

An elephant proposed to her
But she treated him with scorn
And charged off with a rhino
Because the rhino
Had the ...Horn.

The night is still, the moon is full
The clock in the hall strikes two
But no one here will sleep tonight
Until I have told my tale to you.

I am a friendly chicken
Living on a farm
I like peace and quiet
And will do no one no harm.

But all day long
The dog in the yard goes
Woof, WOOF, Woof.
Woof, WOOF, Woof.

All day long that dog .
In the yard goes.
WOOF, WOOF, WOOF!
And the cows in the field go.
...MOO!

And the duck in the pond goes
Quack, QUACK, Quack!
Quack, QUACK, QUACK!
All the long day through.

All day long
The dog goes WOOF
And the duck goes quack
And the cows in the field go moo.

So when they settle down to sleep
I go...

Cock A DOODLE DOO!

UGH!

Yesterday I went to bed 'cause I was in great pain.
No sooner had I got in bed than I was out again.
Now I like horses
I like dogs
And I like sheep, and deer!

But I will not stay in bed
With a cat!
With diarrhoea!

THE CAT AND THE POND

I saw this little tadpole, as it changed into a frog.
It jumped out of the water and settled on a log.
I thought "That looks very tasty, I'll have some of that."
A frog is a nice tit bit
For me...I am a pussy cat.

I stretched out a paw to catch it and before I could stop
I fell in the water 'cause the frog, it did a hop.
Well now I'm here to tell you of frogs I am not fond
Because I am a poor old pussy cat
Drowning in this pond!

TROUSERS

I can't find my trousers! So my trousers I can't don
And I can't go to work until I've got some on.
I took them off last night and laid them on the chair
And now they've gone and vanished.
They are simply just not there.

Oh! Where on earth have they gone?
I've thought and thought and thought.
They can't have walked off on their own
At least they shouldn't ought.

I still can't find my trousers
And I've got to go to work
But if I go without them
I'll look a proper berk.

I have looked in the bathroom
And I've looked in the hall,
But I can't find my trousers
There's no sign of them at all.

I'm on my way to work now
Off to work I've gone.
I have found my trousers
I already had them on!

SPLAT!!

I awoke this morning with an awful fright
As I saw how the little thing I had
Had grown big over night.

I showed it to my sister Marge
And she yelled out,
"Cor! I've never see another one
As big as that before!"

I showed it to the doctor and he said,
"If that!Grows much bigger
You'll have to buy a hat."

From that doctors treatment
I really did recoil
'Cause he pulled out a great big lance
And with it slashed my boil.

SPLAT!

FISH

I found myself a cosy nook
And settled by a babbling brook
The sun was shining in the sky
And from the corner of my eye

I saw the way the gentle breeze
Moved the leaves upon the trees
In the leaves of burnished gold
I saw a sight to behold.

A kingfisher of blue so bright
Sat so still, then took to flight
The sky was filled with dazzling hues
Of whites and pinks and brilliant blues.

Content and happy I sat there
And watched enthralled as a pair
Of foxes frolicked in the sun
Tails held high and full of fun.

So peaceful did I feel inside
It felt so good I almost cried
I set my rod and cast my hook
Far into the babbling brook.

As the sun set in the sky
And the clouds rolled slowly by
I felt a spot of gentle rain
And even then did not complain.

When darkness came, I still sat there
And felt a nip come in the air.

I watched the leaves upon the trees
Turn to white as they did freeze
Did I complain? Not at all
Not even when the snow did fall.

The moon and stars shone in the sky
And lost in space I realised why.

At one with nature we should live
And enjoy the treasures it does give.

I finished up my bottle of gin
And decided I must turn it in
I felt my muscles tense and cramp
And shivered from the cold and damp.

I'd fished all day and fished all night
And never had one single bite
So I went home without a fish
And oh how I sincerely wish
I had never seen that blasted place!

FOR JOY

I can move a mountain
I can paint the sky
I can swim an ocean
Drain the rivers dry.

But I can't live without you.
Baby please, don't die.

> Oh! My Joy, my darling.
> Oh! My Joy, my wife.

> For you I'll give my soul.
> My heart, my mind, my life!

Every night I'm praying
The Lord will make you well.
Then I'll build him a stairway
And I'll block the gates of Hell!

So now you know my darling
How much you mean to me

> Let's go scale a mountain
> Let's go sail the Sea!

Now that I have lost you
Now that death has won

> My sorrow shades the moon
> My tears have doused the sun.

I can't go on living
I just want to die
Then we can move the Heavens
And we will walk the sky.

WINTER'S DAY

On a summer night long, long ago
as the moon it shone like gold
A woman said she loved me
and together we grew old

On an autumn evening as the sun sank from the sky
And autumn leaves of burnished gold fluttered down to die
My woman said she loved me, and with a soft and gentle
sigh
Her eyes fluttered like those autumn leaves
and she laid down to die

Now my life's like a winter's day
my heart is as cold as snow
And I wonder when my living's done, will my soul go
to that summer's night of long ago

And will we
love together
for all eternity.

ENGLISH ROSE

She was a lovely English Rose living in our town
She had a winning smile and seldom wore a frown
One day a friend scoffed at her, "You really are so plain,"
And from the day that was said, she never was the same.

Now her lips are painted crimson
Her eyes thick with black
Her hair is cropped and stubbed
Tattoos all down her back.

She was a lovely English Rose who seldom wore a frown
Now she seldom smiles and looks just like a clown.

MADNESS

There`s a madness about me on this autumn day
As I hear birds singing and see squirrels at play
There's a madness about me, this cannot be right.
Me? Enjoying these woods, where it`s peaceful and quiet.

I`m loud and I`m brash, I`m a man of the world.
By this sort of thing my attentions not held.
There's a madness about me, do you hear what I say.
There's a madness about me on this autumn day.

I live in the fast lane, I've no time to relax.
I've a car to pay for and a mortgage, and tax.
What's he doing looking at me that blackbird up there
In this beautiful tree?

Is it the sunlight dancing on leaves
That's filling my mind so full of ease?
I must get away. There is work to be done.
I've no time for all this. I've no time for fun.

I should be elsewhere at work, or the club.
Where I am the Big Wheel. The centre; the hub!
There is peace and contement here in this wood.
I can't feel this happy. I can't feel this good!
There's a madness about me. Its blowing my mind.
I'm feeling so loving. I'm feeling so kind.
I'm feeling its life as I lean on this tree.
There are tears in my eyes...There`s a madness in me.

There's a madness in me, its holding me here.

54

There's an owl in this tree and look there's a deer.
As I squat and lean on this tree.
My mind is now clear and now I can see.

There's no madness about me so now I can leave.
I'm at peace and contented now I believe.
There's no madness about me, as I walk to my car.
And gaze at the moon. And follow a star.

There's no madness about me. I no longer feel odd.
There is peace all about me. I'm close to my God.

A WALK IN THE WOODS

If my friend you cannot find
Inspiration in your mind
I'm sure my friend that you could
By strolling with me in a wood.
And see the burnished golden leaves
Flutter in the evening breeze.
Blackbirds singing in a tree
Are such a lovely sight to see.
Bluebells carpeting the ground.
Move with the breeze, but make no sound.
Squirrels munching from their paws.
Owls on branches, cling with claws.

Roe deers hear the blackbird's song.
Sense us there, and they are gone.
An old oak tree knurled and knotted.
Toadstools standing plain and spotted.
Bushes laden down with fruit.
The old wise owl gives out a hoot.
A beaver in a coat of stripes.
Acorns sitting in their pipes.
A fox creeps back into his den.
A magpie's quill to make a pen.
Moss covers dead wood here and there.
The old fox snoring in its lair.
There's so much more for us to see.
Come and walk the woods with me.

THE MAN IN THE MOON

He appears every month with a smile on his face
Wearing ears, no clothes, oh what a disgrace!
But let's not condemn him at least not too soon
The man with the smile is the man in the Moon.

BIG BRAVE INDIAN

He was a big brave Indian, that cannot be denied.
He told me how his people lived and why his people died.
Strangers came to live with them and created pain and strife.
They plundered the resources, and destroyed a way of life.

They destroyed a way of life that spanned ten thousand
years.
And drove the people from their land, along a trail of tears.
Mothers, brothers, sisters, all walked hand in hand.
And died along that trail, mourning for their land.

They drove then to a barren land, where the corn seed
would not grow.

They told them they could live on meat, then slew their
buffalo.

But he was a big brave Indian that cannot be denied.
He returned to his land to live for those that died.

But the strangers would not let him live, not on his
homeland.
They told him he must live elsewhere, but he did not
understand.

So they tied him to an old oak tree and whipped him with
their guns. Then raped and slew his sons.

But he was a big brave Indian and he refused to cry.
So they tore his heart out with a knife and threw it down to dry.

And as the sun grew higher in the midday heat.
That heart began to beat!

It was beating out a rhythm
Counting out a toll
Asking its creator to damn the white man's soul!
There are those that said that Indian had no right to live.
Who hear that heart a beating and beg it to forgive.

For it beats throughout the universe
with hope and strength and pride.

The heart of that brave Indian who's spirit never died

MARSHAL LAW

He rode into town early evening
And went for a drink at the bar
The barman he poured him a whisky
And a woman she polished his star.

The Marshal had come for a showdown
With a gunman called Danny Magrew
But Danny was wise and was clever
So he called to the woman he knew.

The woman she worked in a whorehouse
They called her 'Old Sexy Lill'
To her Danny said "Take him to bed
And soften him up for the kill."

The woman she winked at the Marshal
And into her bed did entice
He dived in and out very quickly
'Cause the bed it was crawling with lice.

He picked up his boots and his saddle
And down to the bar quickly fled
He gulped down a quick double whisky
And turned to Danny and said...

"You set me up with that woman,
You dirty son of a bitch!
How can I have a showdown with you,
When my hands are all blotchy and itch?"

Old sexy Lill was stark naked
And felt like an object of scorn.
She ran down the stairs with a trumpet
And gave the Barman the horn.

"You Bastard!" She yelled at the Marshal
"You tried to take me by force!"
And the Marshal jumped up on his saddle
And rode out of town on his horse.

When the Marshal's hands stopped itching
He quickly road back into town
And there he went looking for Danny Magrew
Intending to gun the man down.

Old Lill she spotted the Marshal
And ran to her Danny to tell.
Now Danny Magrew was a frightened
Old Lill she could tell by the smell.

The Marshal he crashed through the swing doors
And all in the bar, they stood still
As he pointed his gun at Danny Magrew
The man he had vowed he would kill.

Danny stood there with fear in his eyes
And his hands did tremble and quiver.
Then the Marshal he froze as a gun touched his nose
With old Lill at the end of its trigger.

"Put down your gun!" She demanded
As Danny did sigh with relief.
"Put down your gun!" She demanded once more,
"Or mine will fill you with grief!"

The Marshal he lowered his six gun

And he spat, and he cussed, and he swore.
Danny Magrew had been saved once again
By old Lill the town's sexy whore.

"You don't deserve a woman like that!"
He growled at Danny Magrew.

Then old Lill fired the gun at his crotch,
And the Marshal was then minus two.

Now Danny and Lill they got married
And a fine young family did raise.
The Marshal he walks into town now and then
And just stands around in a daze.

A man may be quick on the trigger
And out of his saddle stand tall
But a man who will scorn old sexy Lill
Will do no riding at all.

MY ODE TO JOY

I tried to write a poem
So all the world could see
Just how wonderful you were
And how much you meant to me.

So I searched through the thesaurus
And I searched the dictionary
But there were no words that could convey
How much you meant to me.

So I tried to paint your picture
So all the world could see
Just how beautiful you were
And how much you meant to me,

But there has never been an artist
In all of history
That could portray your beauty
Or how much you meant to me.

So I tried to write your music
But there is no melody
That could captivate the way you were
Or how much you meant to me.

But I don't have to write a poem
Or no melody.
I don't have to paint a picture
Because the angels all can see

Just how beautiful you are
And how much you mean to me.

WEDDING DAY

Oh I looked so smart on my wedding day
In my top hat and my new suit of grey
I looked so smart so smart and so neat;
From the top of my head
To the soles of my feet.
It was a hot, a hot summer's day
The day I got married
In old Galway Bay.

Inside the church we all felt the heat
And then came the smell
The smell from my feet.
The Vicar turned blue
And the service did fluff.
And my bride's mother ran off in a huff.

My bride blushed and cried out in shame
When the whole congregation, they did the same.
The wedding reception it did not fare well
No one would eat there because of the smell
They drank all the drink, but no one would eat
Because of the smell
The smell from my feet!

For a hotel room her father did pay
For me and my wife on our wedding day
I sit there alone, so lonely and sad
As I yearn for the wife, that I've never had
Into my bed my wife did not come
She'd packed her bags and gone home to her mum.

When I took my shoes off and threw them away
I killed all the fishes in old Galway Bay
I'm the only one left here, I'm sorry to say
Since I took my socks off on my wedding day

WOODPECKERS

They talk a lot of Noah and his ark and how for forty days
and nights they floated in the dark, but what about old Jed
the other bloke, whom on God played a really wicked joke.

"Go and build an Ark," God told him, "Go and build one
big and strong, because soon I will flood the world with
water, water that an ark can float upon."

Well, Jed he did the same as Noah, he built a great big
blooming Ark, and filled it up with animals, and birds,which
he took for a lark

When the rains came down and the world began to flood,
the birds began sing and the cows, they chewed the cud.

For thirty days, days as black as night, when not one inch of
land appeared in sight, in that ark upon the water, birds did
things they didn't oughta, which later caused a very sorry
plight.

When the rains subsided and the water it did calm,
"The ark is sinking Lord!" Jed cried loudly in alarm.

And then the Lord he sighed, and said in a voice soft and
kind,
"You did the best you could, but in an Ark that's made of
wood, you should have left the woodpeckers behind".

DANIEL

Daniel, a runaway slave, hid himself in side a cave
He heard a growl and it was then, he knew it was a lion's
den.

The lion it just laid there whimpering on the floor
Licking at a thorn imbedded in its paw.
Daniel felt real sorry for that lion, so forlorn
And with his thumb and finger he removed the thorn.

So grateful was the lion to be free from pain
At last he let young Daniel go, and so the die was cast.

In a cage in ancient Rome, a lion's mouth did drip with
foam
Left for weeks without meat a Christian he was fed to eat.
Freed from his cage at long last, he had the chance to break
his fast
That lion crept out like a spaniel and licked the hand of poor
old Daniel

And as he did Daniel saw, the scar upon the lions paw.
They gazed into each others eyes, and to Daniel's great
surprise
As he went to try and pet him
The lion jumped up and then it ate him.

JONAH

Jonah was a bloke that got swallowed by a whale
He was the only one that knew that
So who told told Jonah's tale?

Well Jonah did himself
Of that there is no doubt
The whale did not eat him
It shot him out its spout.

From the crows nest of a ship
A sailor he did spy
Jonah shoot up in the air
As he went soaring high.

The sea was calm as Jonah
Crashed down on that ships sail
And that's why old Jonah lived
To tell this fishy tale.

TUSK

Today my Son we are to study the ways of the most
magnificent creature on Earth.

For we must know the ways of our potential prey.
We will see that although he is the largest of all creatures
He is feared by none, for he hunts nothing but leaves and
fruits.

"No my Son, his carcass will not feed us, though the winter
for his flesh is tough and has a bitter taste that dries the
mouth
and one swallow sickens the stomach for days.
No we will not hunt him for his hide, for his skin is rough
and unbending and can not be fashioned into garments or
shelters".

"See how he bathes in the dust, how he whirls and twills.
Then hear the trumpet sound he makes. That is his way of
showing the world how happy he is just to be alive.
See how he snuggles close to his mate, and how his children
love him.

      Why do we hunt him?
      See his tusk!"

NO SHOES

I COMPLAINED BECAUSE I HAD NO SHOES
THEN I CHANCED TO MEET
A MAN WHO WAS A BEGGING
A MAN WHO HAD NO FEET.

MY POOR OLD HEART IT LIFTED
AND AWAY FLEW ALl MY BLUES
I SAID 'YOU GOT NO FEET MATE'
SO CAN I HAVE YOUR SHOES?'

HE LOOKED AT ME AND SHOOK HIS HEAD
THOUGHT A BIT AND THEN HE SAID...

'You are either on the drugs mate
Or you've been on the booze
What would I be doing
With a pair of shoes?'

I said, 'I'm very sorry mate
It really is a shame
Perhaps I'll come and join you
In this begging game.'

He said, 'Oh no you won't mate
Me you will not mock,
I might not have feet or shoes
But I will give you a sock!'

I said, 'Don't be like that mate
I'm worse off than you's

You ain't got no feet
So you didn't need no shoes.'

He looked at me and scratched his head
Thought a bit and then he said…

'You ask anyone
Anyone you choose
Would they sooner have no feet
Than to have no shoes?'

Well I suppose I'm better off than him
If you take it on the whole
I knew he couldn't chase me
So I pinched his begging bowl.

Yeah! I pinched his begging bowl
And down the road I scoots
Then ran into a charity shop
And bought myself some boots.

I suppose you think I'm rotten,
But I don't give two hoots
'Cause I'm looking for a beggar man
Who has no use for suits.

INTRODUCING CASEY JONES

Young Casey left his home
To set off in a quest
To search for gold and silver
In 'The Wild West'.

At sixty-six old Casey Jones
Muscles cramped and aching bones
In fruitless quest, like men untold
Discovered not one ounce of gold.

His youth all spent his spirit down
Casey yearned for his home town
Over barren lands he'd roam
Searching, searching for his home.

Weak, feeble, his memory gone
Dear old Casey staggered on.
In another forlorn quest
To get back home there to rest.

*****

An old man walks a railroad track
Praying it will take him back
To the town where old, old Casey Jones
Can go home to lay his bones.

He is looking kinda feeble
And is moving really slow

'Cause he don't know where he came from
So he don't know where to go.

And as the trains go speeding by
You can hear them mournfully cry

Choo-Choo train! Where am I heading to?
I am lost and all alone. Choo-Choo train
Where are you going to? Choo-Choo train
Take me home.

He don't know if he'll make it
But he sure is going to try
To get back to the town he loves
It's there he wants to die.

Over barren lands he'll roam
Searching, searching for his home.

His knees are bent and buckled
And his throat is parched and dry
He knows he will never make it
But he still is going to try.

And as the trains go speeding by
You can hear his feeble cry
Choo-Choo train. Where are you going to?
Must I die here all alone?
Choo-Choo train. Where are you going to?
Choo-Choo train. Take me home.

And as the vultures circle high
Casey knows it's time to die.
And when he hears the angels call
Poor old Casey takes a fall.

And as the vultures circle down
In his dreams, he's in the town
And there the sun will bleach the bones
Of poor, poor old…
Casey Jones!

SAINT?

I was happily married to a woman who was a saint.
I'd like to say that I still am, but I'm sorry to say that I ain't.
I lusted after an angel as she played on her harp in the park.
And I made love to that angel as the world grew misty and dark.

I fell asleep with that Angel as she sang a sweet, sweet love song
And when I awoke in the morning, her harp and her wings they had gone.

I looked in the eyes of that angel
And they had turned to blood red.
Her teeth had grown like the fangs of a wolf
And two horns popped out of her head.

That sweet, sweet feminine angel
Had turned to a devil…a male!
He looked at me with a leer on his face
And flicked me to Hell with his tail.

So if like me you are married
Don't! Don't ever stray
Because what may look like an angel
Could well be a devil at play.

KILLER

I used to be so fit and strong, a proper macho man
I'd laugh and drink, and fight and smoke like any young
man can.

But now I'm weak and feeble and have to stay in bed
No strength within my arms and legs, and not a hair upon
my head.

This thing that grows inside me, it gets bigger every day
But because I smoked tobacco it's the price I have to pay.
Tobacco killed my father and it's going to kill me too
But I don't want to die, son, I'm only thirty-two.

But my life is coming to an end; my living's almost done
So you look after Mother, and please! Don't smoke my son.

TREATY

We signed a treaty that said,
On our homeland we stay
For as long as the stars shine in the sky
But, stars don't shine in the day.

The very next day the 'Long Knives' rode in
At the time our braves were away.
They slaughtered our women, children and old
And for that black deed they will pay.

The blood of the 'Long Knives' runs thick on the ground
Their bodies lay dead in the corn.
Not one of those killers survived on that day
At the battle of…
'The Little Big Horn'.

PIG IN A POKE

The other day for a joke
I gave the farmer's pig a poke
I poked it with a stick, not hard
Yet it flew around the yard.

That pig, he did a lot of harm
As he whizzed around the yard
It charged the cows and then a horse
And I got the blame of course.

But I ask, how could I know
How far a poked pig would go?
When it destroyed the chickens' pen
It went and charged the cows again.

It charged the cows
The chickens and sheep
And knocked the farmer
In the dung heap.

All the while there was I
Trying to coax it back in its sty
I had nearly got it back
When on my back I felt a whack.

It was the farmer with a stick
And the smell of him made me sick
Then he chased me with a gun
And oh! Boy did I run.

I tell you now
It is no joke
To give a farmer's
Pig a poke.

STELLA

Stella Simon met a Pie Man going to the fair
Said Stella Simon to the Pie Man
'Let me taste your ware.'
Said the Pie Man to Stella Simon
'Show me first your penny.'
Said Stella Simon to the Pie Man
Kind Sir I have not any.'
Said the Pie Man to Stella Simon
'Well show me your 'ha'penny then!'

PUB SINGER

There's a man who sings in our pub
Who cannot sing a note
His voice can't hold a tune
And the words stick in his throat.

He always starts his singing
When he's been on the beer
That fills the pub with laughter
And the punters stand and cheer.

He dances on the tables
And on the floor he skips
He waves his arms like windmills
And waggles both his hips.

Yes! He dancesf on the tables
And skips upon the floor
And when he stops his singing
The people yell for more.

He is a silly sod that bloke is
With that I must agree
The silly sod that dances here
That silly sod is me.

LOW DOWN RAT BAG

He's…a…Stinking…Lousy…Lowdown
Scheming…Rat Bag!

He's…a…Stinking…Lousy…Lowdown
Sort of bloke!

And when I catch that lousy rotten rat bag…
My finger in his eye I will poke!

Yeah!

When I catch that dirty lousy scum bag

I will show him it ain't no joke.

To steal my car and drink up all my whisky…

All because I gave his wife a poke!

HIAWATHA

Hiawatha he does stalk, with a knife and a tomahawk.
He's a great big Indian chief.
He has plenty wampum.

He will creep up on his foes,
And on their head will bonk 'em.
Hiawatha has a big chopper.
That makes Mini...
HA...HA...!

DEVILS OR GODS

I have some paper and a pen, I'd like to write but don't know when.

When I find the inspiration to write the things that won't shock the nation.

I have some thoughts within my head that would shock, if they were read.

So perhaps I'll just sit here through the night, thinking things I dare not write.

Things that ask why we are at war, and what the hell we are fighting for.

To me it seems rather odd to say we fight in the name of God.

But fight we do and what a shame, we don't fight in the Devil's name.

For it must be the Devil that drives us to kill, so why ask God to foot the bill?

I've heard you say that we are right, in God's name for the Devil to fight.

But I have heard them say the same thing too, so who is right, them or you?

I can't get this thought out of my head. Are they Devils or Gods that lay there dead?

Some things are unjust I know that it is true, but there must be other things we can do.

Other things than to kill and maim, then brag we do it in God's name.

Are they Devils or Gods that lay there dead? There is no

answer in my head.
So I'll leave these thoughts unsaid.

I'll put away my paper and pen, until the Devil or God...
knows when.
When we can all live as one nation and in God's name find
salvation.

DRUGS

If you ask a man why he's hooked on a drug
He will just stare at you and his shoulders will shrug
Because he doesn't know the reason why
He's killing himself and waiting to die.
It's so hard for him in the world that he lives
For him to enjoy the gifts that it gives.
The face that he shows to the world's not his own
He only shows that when he's all alone.
His feelings and spirit are trapped in his head
And will not break free until the day that he's dead.
He started on hash, then grass, then cocaine
To try and break free, free from the pain.
For the man lives in a constant dread and a fear
That is only curtailed and restrained by veneer
And should that start to peel or crack
A man to an animal will quickly turn back.
Yet man is an animal and should be so proud
He should stand on his two feet and shout it out loud,
For he was born of this world and born to be free – not
Shackled or chained and told what to say
But born to enjoy life and live for each day.
But restricted by customs, laws and taboos
He looks for his solace in the drugs and the booze.
Yet if he takes time to look around
He will find in this world good things abound.
There's flowers and trees
And there's birds, and there's bees
There's rivers and mountains and streams
And there's hopes and there's dreams.
Should man wish to break free from his plight

Let him stand and gaze at the stars in the night
And as he gets lost in the stars up above
He will get some strange feelings like hope, trust and love.
He will start to think of the good things in life
Like his parents and friends, his children and wife.
None of these things can be found in a drug
For there's nothing so potent or as desirable as love.

JONNY HAD AN ACCIDENT

Jonny had an accident on the way to Harrow
He broke the bottom off his spine and
Out shot all its marrow.

The doctors had a conference and did all agree
To fill poor Jonny's spine up with some mercury.

In the summertime he's fine
He walks at eight feet tall
But when the winter comes along
He rolls up in a ball.

DO IT YOURSELF ALF

My name's Alf I do it myself but I am not much good
At screwing screws, banging nails or even sawing wood.
When this here Alf built a shelf, it fell off the wall
It landed on my head and bounced just like a ball.

How I did yell, as it fell from my head to foot
I picked it up and threw it down, now the sink's kaput.
So I tried to mend that sink, but I shouldn't have oughta
The tap flew off in my hand and I got soaked in water.

I slipped and slid and knocked the lid, off the old waste bin
I did my best to stop myself but my head got stuck in.
I let out a roar, charged for the door and knocked it off its
hinges
Now I hurt from head to toe and I'm full of aches and
twinges.

With the kitchen deep in water and rubbish floating by
The knob flew off the broken door and hit me in the eye.
Now I'd made my mind up how the water flow I'd stop
So I hit it with my hammer and broke off the cock.

Soaking wet but not beat yet I knew just what to do
I grabbed a turnkey and out to the road I flew.
I turned the water off from there, and went indoors to repair
All the damage I had done to the kitchen of my mum.
My mum large eyed with threatening glare
Quickly kicked me out of there.

It's been like that all my life; I never get no praise

So off I went back home to stay in bed for days.
I asked my wife to join me and she said 'Oh no Alf!
At that you are far too clumsy, just do it yourself.'

MY AMBITION

All my life it's been my ambition
To win a prize in a competition.
I was feeling bored, so for a lark
I thought I'd make a work of art.

So I made a model bird
From two crows feathers
And a dried up turd.

I took my birdie down the Tate
And showed it to the old curate.
'What the hell is that?' he said
Then took a sniff and dropped down dead.

One judge who turned up late
Gave his vote to the dead curate.
The first prize must have been a fix,
Nothing more than a pile of bricks.

Second prize as it came to pass
Was half a cow inside a glass.
Can you guess what came in third?
Two crows feathers and a
Dried up…TURD!

POLKA DOT TIE

The doctors were amazed at the stubbornness of Dan,
For his life had stretched too many years beyond its natural span.
A student of psychology once asked the reason why, and this was Dan's reply:

I don't like my son in law!
He's a most peculiar guy!
He wears a big pair of yellow boots!
A bright pair of red, red sox!
And a great big polka dot tie!
So if he's coming to my funeral
I ain't gonna bloody well...
I ain't gonna bloody well...
I ain't gonna bloody well...
...DIE...

MAY ALL YOUR TROUBLES

May all the troubles you may have
Fade and float away
Now that God's created
A new and glorious day.

May fortune smile upon you in everything you do
And may that smile light up your face
All a long life through.

PIGEON TOES

It stood upon the riverbank
And in the mud it slowly sank.

It lifted up a big black foot and plonked it down again
Then let out a mighty quack
A quack that told the whole wide world
That duck was in great pain.

That poor old great big fat old duck
The poor old silly bugger
Had lifted up one big webbed foot
And stamped on the other.

It lifted up its bottom foot
And over it did fall.
Life for a poor old duck like that
Is no fun at all.

How a duck like that survives
Only Heaven knows.
It must be hell to be a duck,
A duck with pigeon toes.

INSIDE OUT MAN

I am the inside out man
That means there's two of me.
One I keep close to myself
It's the other one you see.

The one I show off to the world
I like to think is cool,
And often just for fun
I like to play the fool.

The one I keep to myself
Is not like that at all.
He may be many other things
But is not a fool.

Because…
Deep within me dwells a tiger.

THE TIGER INSIDE

I am just a simple man
Living life the best I can.
But, I see things in this world
That make me want to yell out loud.

I want to spit and snarl and scream.
But all I do is sit and dream.

Deep within me dwells a tiger
Living all my dreams for me.
And should I set my tiger free
All would doubt my sanity.

But I am just a simple man
Living life the best I can.
Yet as my tiger spits and grows
I feel him tearing at my bowels.

I hear him talking in my head
Words that I must leave unsaid.
Because if I let him speak for me
All would doubt my sanity.

So I close my eyes to all about me
Shut my mind to poverty.
I block my ears to those that tell me
'Hugger kills.' And will not see.

Old folk crying, freezing, dying.
Young ones striving helplessly.

Deep within me dwells my tiger
Strong and filled with honesty.
Sleeping, dreaming, longing
Waiting, waiting, to be free.

As my tiger wakes and growls
I feel him stirring in my bowels

But I am just a simple man
Living life the best I can.

Deep within me snarls my tiger
Eating at the heart of me.
And my mind is full of anger
As I strive for sanity.

Leaders strong and worldly wise
Do not cheat or tell us lies.
For they are blessed with integrity
And know much more than you or me.

But leaders claim that to protect us
From some wicked enemy
We must pay a price for freedom
In the name of liberty.

With old folk dying, young ones crying
Sick ones waiting hopelessly.

Deep within me growls a beast
That I restrict to keep the peace .
Because I am such a simple man
I should do the best I can

To...

Unite the nations set them free
To end all wars and poverty.
Feed the hungry? House the homeless?
Give the sick some dignity?

Provide for children and old folk too?
Is my tiger deep in you?

Must we set our tigers free
To restore our sanity

That's what my tiger asks of me.

But I am just a simple man
Living life the best I can.

But simple one day I will not be
When I set my tiger free.

NOBLE TIGER

Imagine if you can
A quiet clearing
All is still and peaceful
Save for a whisp of wind
That hardly stirs
The lush green grass
Stretched on all fours.

Sprawling lies a basking tiger
At peace and in
Harmony with his world
The coat of the tiger
Is sleek and colourful
Contentment oozing
From his being
Watch him raise his head
And growl a harmless growl
That lasts no time at all as
A butterfly flies by
Watch his head roll down
As graceful as the Condor.

How happy is our tiger with none to steal his space or rouse
him to anger.
Watch as he stretches elegant and graceful, then hear the
contented groan
As he lolls upon the Mother Earth.
See the tiger plod with purpose. See him pause then bare his
fangs in silent preparation for the hunt.
Watch the tiger stalk...see the muscles ripple.

See the power...see the tiger run...see the tiger leap.
How beautiful in his stripes a living rhapsody of strength
and power, or beauty and grace.
See him pounce...watch him...watch him bare his teeth.
See the pride and dignity he brings to the kill!
How noble is our tiger.

THE SMILE ON THE FACE OF THE WIDOWER

I went to the pub early evening; I thought I'd just stay for a while
There was a guy all alone in a corner, on his face a peculiar smile.
So I winked at the barman and pointed, and he said through gritted teeth
'Leave that old guy alone in his corner, or he'll bore you to death with his grief.'

But a pub is no place for the lonely, so I went to that man with the smile
And he said, 'As we're both on our own mate, perhaps we could talk for a while.'
Well I stayed in that pub all the evening, and learned so much of his life
He told me how lonely he'd been since he lost his darling sweet wife.

There was a smile on the face of that widower that made him look like a silly old man.
There's a hurt in the heart of the widower that cripples as only grief can.
There's a look in the eye of the widower that's hiding a river of tears.
There is a scar on the soul of the widower that will bleed for the rest of his years.

There's a lilt in the voice of the widower as he speaks of the days of gone by

102

But the look in the eye of the widower is saying, 'I just want to die.'

There's a wish in the mind of the widower, and that is someday he **will** die.

And then he will be united with his wife in Heaven that's **why**!

There's a smile on the face of the widower!

MOO...LA...HA

(Mother Earth)

On a lonely evening while gazing at a star
I heard a voice whisper...

'My name is Moo...La...Ha...
If you care to walk with me
I will take you by the hand
And show you all my treasures
My sky, my sea, my land'
And as I walked along with her
Over land and seas
She spoke to all the animals
The fishes and the trees.
And it was oh so beautiful.
Beautiful...beautiful.

She showed me many, many things.
That I had seen before
I had looked at them so often
But never really saw.
The glory of creation.
The wonder of a tree.
The miracle of living.
The rhythm of the sea.
And it was oh so beautiful.
Beautiful...beautiful.

She took me to a mountain top
And kissed the stars above.

And there she did encompass me
With overwhelming love.
A love for all creation.
A love for all the trees.
For everything that's living
The rhythm of the seas.

We stayed upon that mountain top
Until the break of dawn.
Where she told me of the reason
The reason I was born

'You must attend my treasures
My sky, my sea, my land.
And walk among your people
And make them understand!'

'That I am their Earth Mother
I give them all they need.
But, they are slowly killing me
With selfishness and greed.
And I am oh so beautiful.
Beautiful...beautiful.'
And as she turned to leave me
These words came to my head.
They came from deep within my soul
And this is what they said...

Moo..La...Ha ...
You are beautiful.
I love you more than life
More than just a brother.
A mother or a wife.
Moo...La...Ha...
You are beautiful
Beautiful to see.

You gave all your treasures
To love and nurture me.

And when my living's over
When my life is done.
You will take me to your heart
Just like a newborn son.
But before my living's over
I will do all I can.

To protect you...Mother Earth.
From that animal...
Called MAN!

WHEN? WHEN? WHEN?

When Mother Nature and her husband 'The Sun' created the Heavens they divided their wondrous powers and treasures, among their children, the Gods.

When the Mother of all learned her children were fighting over their possessions she took all of the treasures and placed them in the heart of the Sun.

The God's were very angry and blamed each other for their Mother's deed, so they fought even more. Such was their wrath they plundered the resources, and produced terrible weapons of destruction.

When the Mother of all learned from her two surveying children that the rest had been turned to dust by those terrible weapons, she wept.

'If it takes forever,' she told her son and daughter, ' I will create a world where all can live in peace and harmony'.

When she removed the treasures from the heat of the heart of the father she molded them into a ball. Tenderly she bounced it on her breast and nurtured it with love.

Carefully she made her plans.
Lovingly she weaves her tapestry of life.
Gently she hugged and kissed it until it was so full of love it rose from her hand's and floated into space.

When the two Gods gazed upon the thing their Mother had

fashioned from her treasures – a seething mass of hellfire and molten rock, heaving and slivering as it spat and gurgled – they wept for their Mother.

When the tears of the Gods fell on the blazing ball of fire, creating steamy vapors, clouds formed and floated to the Heavens.

When the clouds shed their water to douse the hellfire of earth, tiny specks of cosmic dust came down with the rain.

When water cooled the Earth and flowed through nooks and crannies it filled craters, formed rivers and seas.

In the seas, tiny specks of cosmic dust moved to the slow easy motion of the stars, ebbing and flowing to the rhythm of life.

When the Gods laughed at the antics of the remains of their brothers and sisters their breath caused great winds to howl and rage across the Earth, which carried tiny cell's of cosmic dust from the water to the land.

When deprived of their source of life and motion those cell's contracted and shredded into fibrous spores that clung to the earth waiting.
Waiting for rain.

When nurtured by rain and captured by soil the spores stretched and strained in an attempt to return to the stars.

When grasses grew Mother Nature's cheeks puffed with pride and as her breath sent the Earth spinning on its axis other life dells were sent skimming from the waters.

They, hopped, jumped or floated from blade to blade

absorbing dew from the green.
Green grasses.

When the Earth was covered in grasses and trees
When birds flew and reptiles roamed the Earth Mother
Nature ordered her son and daughter to live on Earth.

Nurse it
Tend it and love it.

'There,' she told them I have hidden all the treasures of
the past. All the beauty of the future and all the love of my
heart.

They are yours to discover use and return to me. Now,' she
went on ,' you must harness it and take it to a place where
your Father, the Sun, can smile gently upon it'.

When the God's Adam and Eve whose tears produced the
waters of life, have learned their Mother's secrets, solved
her mysteries and taught her ways to all the creatures of the
Earth

When they can prevent mankind producing weapons of
mass destruction and plundering the Earths reso urces.

When they can prevent mankind contaminating the air and
polluting Earth's life-giving waters.

When man can love the Earth as he love his Mother's heart
beat.

When they can return to Mother Earth all that is hers.

When they can understand to love the Earth is not to own it.

When they can shout to the Gods
'This Earth is ours for living'.
Then they can fly to the stars and dance to the rhythm of
Life!'

But
When
When.
When?

EYE NOSE

That guy standing there
With his nose in the air
He used to live next door
But me, he chooses to ignore.

But I knows, I knows
I knows, I knows
I knows, I knows
'e knows I

And 'e knows, 'e knows
'e knows, 'e knows
'E knows, I knows, knows he.

When I was at school
He treated I cruel
He used to make I cry.

So if I punch him in the eye
Then he'll know, he'll know
Why.

DON'T BLAME ME

A politician of great renown
An answer to all problems he has found.
He will take the praises all the night and day
But if things go wrong you will hear him say

You can blame it on the people that you meet
You can blame it on the lamppost in the street
You can blame it on the fishes in the sea.

But don't, don't, don't!
Blame me.

OH NO!

He was playing his piano, just the other day
He banged the lid down very hard.
And then I heard him say...

Oh!...NO!...Oh!...NO!
This piano has no doe!
It has 'C' It has an 'E'
It has a La and So!
But like a bankrupt

Ba...k..er!

This piano has no dough!

FRED

I know a bloke, a bloke named Fred
Who is bald and toothless
And with his wife, his wife in bed
Fred was blooming useless.

One day his wife, she said to Fred
'I am going to nag yer
Until you go to the doctors
And come back with viagra'.

He came back with viagra pills
And said 'Darling I have two
I'll take one myself tonight
The other one's for you'.

Fred lay upon his bed that night
He lay there tall and proud
He raised both fist up in the air
And yelled out long and loud,
'I want a WOMAN!'.

His wife she woke up from her sleep
And with a loud and joyous cry
Yelled...
'So do I!
So do I!
So do I !'

SITTING BY A MOUNTAIN

Sitting by a mountain stream
Breathing in the fresh crisp clear morning air.
The thoughts of the mind are as the crystal clear waters of
the stream.

They gurgle and flow in joyous harmony, reflecting the awe-
inspiring, glory of God's creation.

The crystal clear clarity of the mind
and the oneness with nature, allow the whole being to become
lost as all the sprits become one.

The sun and the sky.
The moon and the stars.
The earth and the sea.
The wind and the rain.

All of creation and all the creatures that ever lived are joined
in one glorious rhapsody of
LIFE!

LOVE'S LIKE THIS

It's forty years ago that we got married
Forty years ago that we got wed
I have something I want to say dear
Things I cannot leave unsaid.

I can't paint the picture on a canvas
The picture I see clearly in my mind
I can't describe the way that I am feeling
Such words are far to hard to find.

If I could paint the way that I am feeling
If I could find the words to let you see
The picture that my mind holds of you dear.
The one of love for all eternity.

You are the one that makes life worth living.
You are the one I'll dream of all my life.
You are the one that fills my heart dear.
You are my hope, my love
MY LIFE!

POET'S CORNER

Don't bury me in poet's corner
With Byron, or with Keats.
I've done nothing in my life
To equal their great feats.

Wordsworth wrote of daffodils.
And Brooks did write of wars.
I just write of smelly feet
And knees with scabby sores.

My poems are all wrote in fun
No secret message there in.
I send them to the publishers
They send them to the bin.

So don't bury me in poet's corner
With all those men well read.
Don't put me down with them
At least not until I'm dead.

POINTER DOG

He stood on three legs
That pointer dog;
Tail in the air and as still as a log.

A thin-faced fellow, a well-dressed man
Fired a shot gun
Bang, bang, bang!

Quack went the duck, as it fell from the air
'Fetch!' Yelled the man.
'There, there, there!'

Off went the dog as fast as it could
Straight through the meadow and into the wood.

Back came the dog, quite pleased with himself
A gleam in his eye, and the duck in his mouth.
So pleased with himself that his tail wagged faster
As he lay the duck at the feet of his master.

To the man's surprise
The duck was not dead.
'Cause it flew in the air
And shit on his head.

FAT DUCK

It stood upon the river bank
And in the mud it slowly sank.

It lifted up a big black foot and plonked it down again
Then let out a mighty quack
A quack that told the whole wide world
That duck was in great pain.

That poor old great big fat old duck
The poor old silly bugger
Had lifted up one big webbed foot
And stamped on the other.

It lifted up its bottom foot
And over it did fall.
Life for a poor old duck like that
Is no fun at all.

How a duck like that survives
Only Heaven knows.
It must be hell to be a duck
A duck with pidgin toes.

NEW LAMB

There is nothing in this life so sweet
Than to hear a newborn lamb's first bleat.
For soon that lamb will be a sheep
And grow a coat that's soft and deep.

Then wool provide for me to knit
As at my fireside I do sit.
I knit contented knowing that
My lamb had grown so big and fat.

From its first bleat I just knew.
That lamb would make a lovely stew.

SOMETHING

There are somethings that I'm good at, and some things that
I'm not.

There is one thing that I'm good at, that you may not like a
lot!

There is one thing that I'm good at, and I'm not ashamed to
tell.

Is making funny noises and pretending they don't smell!

Sometimes I do them soft, sometimes I do them loud.
When I done one at Wimbledon I paralysed the crowd.

Sometimes I do them soft, sometime I do them hard.
I done one at Aintree once, that killed a horse at fifty yard!

SOME OF MY POEMS

Some of my poems read like a crime, I can't get them to flow or reason, or rhyme.

I read them out loud and get such a pain that I tear them all up and start them again.

But with this one I'm afraid you've been clobbered.
I could sort it out, but I just can't be bothered!

I just can't be bothered to sort it all out, so where it don't rhyme you will just have to shout.

This one's about a farmer named Dickens, who was trying to sell a deaf man a chicken.

How do you sell a deaf man a chicken? Yell!

'Do you want to buy a chicken?'

That is the end of my rotten poem, so don't punch me up.
I'm going
I'm going!

DREAM SONG

I dreamed last night, I was singing a song!
I dreamed last night, I was singing a song!
And in my dream, my friends all tagged along
And joined me singing!
Singing that song.

We marched down the street
Singing that song!

We marched down the street
Singing that song.

And as we marched
Some others came along
And joined us singing
Singing, that song.

There was hundreds of people, singing one song
Hundreds of people
Singing one song

And as we sang
Others came along
And joined us singing
Singing our song.

There was thousands of people!
Singing one song.
Thousands of people
Singing one song.

And all those people, brought their friends along
Then hundreds of thousands
Were singing one song!

There was hundreds of thousands!
Singing one song
Hundreds of thousands
Singing one song

And as they sang
Still others, tagged along
And millions of people were singing one song

Millions of people were singing one song
Millions of people were singing one song
And all those millions
Brought their friends along

Then the whole world was singing
Singing, one song!

With the whole world singing, singing one song
With the whole world singing, singing one song

With the whole world singing! Nothing can go wrong
When the whole World's singing
Singing
Singing one song!

I woke up this morning, everyone had gone
Woke up this morning, everyone had gone.
So all you people
Will you come along, and join me singing
Singing my song!

I LOVE THE WORLD

I love the world and every thing living
I love the land and I love the sea.
I love the world and all of the people
But I wish they would
Listen to me

I see scars on the earth and I blame the people
They've polluted the air and they've poisoned the sea.
Smoke fills the air, the grasses are dying
And there's acid rain falling on trees.

I love them all but some of the people
Are taking much more than they need.
They take everything with no thought of giving.
They're gonna destroy everything living.

And they're too blind to see what they see
And they're too deaf to listen
Too deaf to listen, too deaf to listen
          To me.

They have robbed Mother Earth of all her resources.
They're messing about with nuclear forces.
They're melting the ice and changing the seasons.
They do all these things for their own selfish reasons.

And they're too blind to see what they see
And they're too deaf to listen
Too deaf to listen, too deaf to listen
          To me.

We must give the earth back all of her treasures.
Clean up the land and the seas.

Clear the smoke from the air
And waste from the ocean
And replant all of her trees.

But nothing will grow
Nothing will grow
Nothing will grow
Without seed.

If you can't find a seed in your mind
Or you're too blind to see what you see
Come take a look, a look in the future
And see what's been bothering me.

Birds fall from the air
And as they lay frying
They are fanned
By a nuclear breeze

And acid rains killed
All the trees.

The whole land is dead
Except where it's burning.

There is gas wafting off from the sea
And there is no one to listen
        No one to listen
        No one to listen

            To me.

KING

This world's a great big funny place
It's sometimes hard to tell
If it's inside out and upside down
And back to front as well.

But I would sort the whole world out
And it wouldn't cost a thing.
If I were king
King of the World!

The world would be a better place
I'd teach you all to sing.
If I were king
King of the World!

We would all be singing just one song
Singing it with gusto. Singing it out loud.
If I were king
King of the World!

We wouldn't make no bombs
And all fighting would cease
The world could be a better place
If we all lived in peace.

We would sing and dance and laugh
For hours upon hours.
If instead of making bombs
We stuck to growing flowers.

The world would smell much sweeter
And it wouldn't cost a thing
To make me king
King of the World!

Then wars and all that sort of thing
Would never be allowed
If I were king
King of the world.

But that can never be
That's what I've been told.
The world would never want a king.

Who's only ten years old.

BUT...

If I, were king, King of the World
I'd fulfil all my plans
To get all the people of the world
To hold each others hands.

And it will be so nice
To hear them sing one song
As all the nations in the world
Really get along.

They can keep their own religions
Their customs and taboos
And they would spend one day a year
In each other's shoes.

And I would teach them all
All to understand.
That our whole wide world

Is just one single land.

A land of beauty and of grace
And all mankind is just one race
And you all would walk.
So tall and proud.

If I were king
King of the World!

BAIT

There's a man who lives down our street
Who is young and fit and handsome.
He has a great big ugly wife but
Wouldn't change her for a ransom.

And oh how that man loves to fish
His name is Harry Mangle.
He don't make love, nor smoke or drink
All he does is angle.

And his great big ugly wife
I think her name is Rose
Has a pair of enormous feet
And a wart encrusted nose

But when he talks about her
That's when he confirms
She has no money and she can't cook
But boy, does she have worms!

And because she loves him dearly
She will smile and twitch her rear
Every time that Harry says
'Pass a worm my dear.'

CLING FILM

He went for a walk in the country
By the side of a clear crystal stream
He laid his head on a grass bank
And dreamed a peculiar dream.

She stood at the door of her cottage
Her knickers were down at half mast
She gazed at the man who was sleeping
And with a trill in her voice she did ask:

'Who put the cling film on the loo!
It was a dirty rotten lousy thing to do!
It's not a lot of fun to do a number one!
And I went in and done a number two!'

'And you'd put cling film on my loo.
You dirty rat bag!
When you wake up
I will have murdered you.'

They found him in the river
But the judge he did forgive her
'Cause he'd put cling film on her loo!

The dirty rat bag.

He put cling film on the loo.

She got her own back!
When he put cling film on the loo!

ON YOUR OWN

'We will catch them if we can old chap.
We will catch them if we can.'
Said the fresh faced copper to the poor old man.

'But we have other things to do you know.
We have other things to do.
We cannot spend too much time on the likes of you.

If you have more trouble you call us on the phone
'Cause now you're on your own old chap
Now you're on your own.'

'But! I haven't got a phone,' he said.
'I can't afford a phone. And I'm frightened and I'm lonely.
It's hell to live alone.'

'Can't you come around to see me
To see that I'm all right?
I'm only asking that because
I'm terrified at night.

I've been robbed four times now.
And I'm frightened for my life.
It wouldn't be so bad if I still had my wife.'

'No! We can't come around to see you!
There is a protest planned.
And we are under-manned you know.
We are under manned.
You see the Social Service's they'll help you if they can...

But!
Now you're on your own old chap
You're on your own old man.'

(At'The Social Services')

'We have no funds for telephones
But I'll tell you what we will do
We will send a 'Home Help' to come and visit you.'

'Well that will help, and thank you.
I don't know what to say.'

'That's all right old fellow
Oh! It costs six pounds a day.'

'But! I haven't got no money.
I can't afford to pay.
Is there something you can do, in some other way?'

'We have locks and chains we can provide.
Peep holes and window bars too
But that is all that we can do.'

Locked inside his third floor flat, number ninety-three
An old man shook and trembled as he sat to eat his tea.
He banged his fist and shouted:

'There must be help for me.
I will go and visit
I'll visit my M.P.'

'So you've been robbed four times you say.'
The politician said.
'I'm glad we've had this chat.
Now you can sleep sound in your bed.

I'll make sure of that!'

Police spokesman to M.P.

'We know he has been robbed four times Sir
And it really is a shame
But! We can't guarantee he won't be robbed again.'

Social services to M.P.

'We know he's on his own Sir!
But there is nothing we can do
He has got his locks and bolts, peep holes
And window bars too!'

'I've done my best,' the M.P. said
'I've done my best for you.
But now you're on your own old chap.
I'm sorry but it's true.'

Alone inside his third floor flat he lived a living hell.
Locked and barred
And bolted just like a prison cell.

Inside the council offices all cramped and drained and bent
A book keeper discovered ninety-three had paid no rent!
He wrote out an eviction order and sent it to 'The Court'
The Magistrates approved it
Bailiffs then were saught.

They knocked and shouted at the door
And laughed and giggled as they swore.
When no access they could gain
They called the police and tried again.

With sledges and rams they broke down the door and gazed
at the junk mail piled on the floor.

From that home
That prison cell
There came an awful, putrid smell
.

They found him laying on his bed
Not moving or breathing
Obviously dead!

They broke all the windows
The front and the rear!
To get rid of the smell of the death and the fear.

Neighbours gathered around to see
What went on at ninety-three.
On the news they shed a tear
For a man who'd been dead for almost a year!

'I'll have an enquiry!' The M.P. told
'We really should look after our old!'

'Not up to us,' a police spokesman said
'We work for the living, not for the dead.'

'No fault of ours!' The council did say
'We only knew no rent did he pay.'

'We did our best !' Social Services said
'But, we should have received an S.O.S.
To let us know he was in distress.'

I did not know him but I feel I'm to blame
And that's why my head
Is hanging in shame.

POOR BOY

We took a poor boy from the city
When he was only three
'Cause something in his smile
Just stole the heart from me.

When he was barely seven
He sat upon my knee
And said 'Dad if I were a rich boy
A musician I'd like to be.'

So I scrounged an old piano
And as proud as proud can be
He sat at that piano and he played a melody.

It was a weird and haunting melody.
A weird and haunting melody.

When he was nineteen and she was fifty-three.
The Lord up in Heaven
Took my wife from me.

He said, 'Dad I've lost my mother
And you have lost your wife.
So I will write a symphony
And dedicate it to her life.'

He wrote a sad, but beautiful symphony
With a weird and haunting melody

Now we have been the whole world over.

And what a sight it is to see
Him conduct his orchestra
And play his symphony.

He plays that sad, but beautiful symphony
With its weird and haunting, melody.

But, when I grew much older
And I could hardly see.
I said 'Son it is a hospice
A hospice is for me.'

He said, 'You have been my father since I was only three
And I have gone from rags to riches
But what a poor man I would be
If I left my father alone
'Cause he was old.

To you I owe my fortune
My fame and all my gold
For you I'll give up everything
And nurse you now you're old.'

You've been a kind and loving Dad to me.
A kind and loving Dad to me.'

And now I'm on my death bed and I can clearly see
A vision of my wife
And I can hear her calling me.

And I can hear the angels
Singing in perfect harmony
I can hear those angels
Singing
A beautiful melody.

THE FLY

I was playing on my banjo
When a fly, flew on my nose
So I hit it with my banjo
And in pain I stood and froze.

Then that fly flew off a buzzing
And settled on the window pane
So I hit it with my banjo!
And the fly flew off again.

It flew out the broken window
And landed on my brothers head
So I hit it with my banjo!
And still that fly it was not dead.

My brother stood there opened mouthed
And with a loud an painful cry
'It's all your fault!' He coughed and spluttered
As in his mouth there flew the fly.

'Get it out!' He pleaded with me
'Get it out or I might die.'
And when I went to try and help him
He spat the fly out in my eye!

So I hit it with my banjo!
Now both eyes were black and blue
And still that fly was still alive
'Cause down the road the bugger flew.

Then I chased it with my banjo
Like some weird demented man
Swiping fresh air with my banjo
As up the road I cussed and ran.

The fly it settled on a lamp-post
'Got ya! Got ya!'Out roared I
And that's what broke, my poor old banjo
The blooming lamp-post, not the fly!

Now I play this great big cello!
And if that fly comes on my nose
With two black eyes
And this great big
Cello!

I'd best leave it I suppose...

RECESSION

When I was only twelve years old
We were in recession.
I didn't go to school a lot
But learned this bitter lesson.

The statesmen of our country.
Are very proud and good
So...
Perhaps it's 'cause I'm stupid
That I've never understood.

Why they can go to banquets
At two hundred pounds a head
And sup champagne and oysters
When all we have is bread.

But...
If I don't go to school today
Perhaps I'll get a job
With the bloke that lives next do
Who my dad calls a slob.

It won't be a proper job
He don't do no real work
And he calls my dad a berk.

He says the way Dad suffers
Will destroy his very soul.
He reckons we'd be better off,
If Dad was on the dole.

He may be right, it could be so.
I know my Dad ain't got no dough.

It was my birthday yesterday
I wanted a toy car.
But I got a present –
A tasty Mars bar.

When my dad he gave it me
My mum she swelled with pride
But when I took the gift wrap off
She ran out and cried.

Why did Dad fall down drunk on the kitchen floor
He ain't done that before.
I can't go to school today
'Cause I ain't got no shoes.

Mum can't afford to buy none
Now Dad's gone on the booze.
It's a pity things have got so bad
Because I really love my mum and dad.

I only see the telly when I go round my mate's
They've taken ours away 'cause Dad can't pay the rates
Mum says we'll have to move soon.
'Cause all the money's spent.
And Dad can't get no overtime
So we can't pay the rent.

My dad was crying yesterday
He said he'd got no hope.
It's not like him to do that
He was fiddling with a rope.

We found him in the attic
Hanging from the beams
He had had enough it seems.

My mum is acting very brave
She says that she's alright.
But I can hear her crying
In the middle of the night.

SOUR FACED WOMAN

She was a sour faced woman, tall and stiff and haughty
She looked a lot, lot older but was barely forty.
You'd never think to look at her, she smouldered with desire
To find herself a willing man, to quench her inner fire

But a virgin of her age didn't stand a chance
Until she met a charming man at a village dance.
Although when she had danced with him, she was as stiff as stone
He had chatted merrily, and asked to take her home.

She tried to act as though for her this was quite normal
And told him that he may in a voice, all stern and formal.
He was a rather clean cut man with a friendly open face
And when he kissed her on the lips, her heart began to race.

The moon full. The night was still. Her mind was in a whirl
As for the first time in her life, she was treated like a girl!
On waking in the morning, she gave a hearty sigh
And said; 'That was very nice. I must find another guy.'

In the village hall one night, full of strong, strong liquor
That sour faced old woman, dived upon the Vicar.
'God is love! And love is good!' She cried out with passion.
'For years and years I have abstained, and I'm here to get
my ration!'

' Oh! My dear!' The Vicar cried, his passion so aroused
That he dropped down his trousers as she stripped off her
blouse.

'A mortal sin is what we've done!' The Vicar did complain.
If that's a sin!' The woman cried, 'then I must sin again!'

The butcher and the baker gave way to her desire
The fireman and the policeman, failed to quench her fire.
Two pimply youths, the postman and an old boy on a zimer
The woman took them all back home but not for any dinner.

At sixty-two still full of fire, the woman dished out favour
To every man she ever met
Except her next door neighbour.

A miserable old fellow
A crusty faced old bore.
Complained about the noise she made
Whilst making love next door.

'But I need love!' the woman yelled, 'I'm old and all alone.'
'That's because you're sour faced.' He told the poor old
crone.

'Oh! You nasty man!' she yelled obviously quite vexed
'It would do you good to have some fun.
It's very nice, is sex.'

'I've heard it's nice,' he said to her, and it can be fun
But sex is not love my dear, you can love only one.'

'And who would love a hag like me'
She sniffed in tears of shame
'If there's such a man alive
Kindly speak his name.'

'His name is Charles' the old man sighed
His voice all soft and coy
'He's loved you since you moved next door

When he was just a boy.'

'Oh! My Charles you should have said
Because I felt the same.
For years and years I lived in hope
And from sex I did abstain.'

'Oh my God!' Old Charlie cried
'My manhood's gone to waste.
Because my love for you was so
I've stayed so firm and chaste.'

'Oh!...My Charles...my darling Charles
Come let me show you what you're missing!'

And then she laid old Charlie low
With lots of love and kissing.

'If this is love,' old Charlie said
'Forever we should stay in bed.'

They stayed in bed for two long weeks
Making love and never stopping.
Today they had their final ride
Coupled
In a coffin!

THE BAKER'S SON

The baker's son his name was Sam
He was a lovely chap
He could not walk, he could not run
Because his knees they had no cap.

When he was young, he was so strong
He was so strong and bold
He went out on a cold, cold night
That's how the story's told.

His trousers they were very short
They stopped way above the knees
And on that cold, cold winter's night
His poor kneecaps
Did freeze.

'Please help me Lord!' Poor Sam he cried.
'My life it cannot end
But I will surely freeze to death
On legs I cannot bend'.

With knees locked tight, that winter's night
Sam prayed the snow would stop
But the snow was so relentless
Back home he had to hop.

Sam bounced like a kangaroo
Through the winter snow
How he ever made it home
I really do not know.

'Poor Sam my child,' the baker cried
'Poor Sam where are your knees?'
'They are somewhere out there in the snow
They fell off when I sneezed'.

The baker knew the butcher
The butcher was his mate
And the tale of poor Sam's knees
To him he did relate.

'I'm just the bloke to help you out'
The butcher did declare
Then took the baker to his shop
And showed him something there.

There they were upon the shelf
Lots of kidneys in a row
But still poor Sam he has no knees
Because the baker had no dough.

LAMENT

In the days of the horseless carriage
When great sanctity was placed on marriage
Husbands, there is no dispute
Used a house of ill repute.
Yet little known of that today
Wives for pleasure would, gladly pay.

This sad tale I must now tell
Of how from grace, a woman fell.

She was a woman of distinction.
I was a poor and lonely boy.
One night that woman of distinction
Took and used me for her toy.

She showed me many, many pleasures
All that made my senses soar.
She taught me how to tease and please her
And trained me well to be her whore.

There were many, many women
She would send up to my room.
They came down with smiles of pleasure
She was paid a gold doubloon.

They were rich and high and mighty
All claimed their husband was a bore .
They all gladly paid that woman
To use her toy boy like a whore.

Some were gentle some were vicious.
Some were kind and some were cruel.
They would call and pay again
To use her toy boy like a tool.

I did suffer pangs of torment
At this lack of dignity
But the money that they paid us
Brought a life of luxury.

I was introduced by high born Ladies
To sons of Earls that they had wed.
No trace of guilt from those Ladies
That I had pleasured in my bed.

There were parties, fun and laughter
Crystal bowls and chandeliers.
Kings and Queens, and Lords and Ladies
Partied here for years and years.

A jealous husband chanced to catch me
Underneath his ladies gown.
She did tell of all the others.
We were driven from the town.

Men did come with burning torches
Once our secret had been learned.
At our home they threw those torches
And danced with pleasure as it burned.

We were hounded to exhaustion
Everywhere we were put to shame.
None would give us food or shelter
Once they heard my Lady's name.

We had gone to rags from riches

Were turned away from every door.
For many years we stayed together
That high class Lady and her whore.

In those hard times we stayed together
Living from those rich ones' bins.
Then one cruel and bitter winter
We paid dearly for our sins.

She fell ill and I did nurse her
In a ditch we found to hide.
There my woman said she loved me
Said she loved me...
Then, she died.

I must have known a score of women
But not one I'd place above
That well known woman of distinction
The only one I'll ever love.

Now I am old and very lonely.
She is six feet underground.
I am cold and oh so hungry
Who will buy me for...
A pound?

THOUGHTS?

Where do thoughts come from and where do they go?
I've asked that question,and still I don't know.

Do they float on the wind and come down with the rain
Then soak their self down deep in the brain?

Do they hide in the memory and lay undisturbed
Then quietly whisper until they are heard?

And once they've been heard where do they go?
I've thought and I've thought and still I don't know.

But!Wherever they came from and wherever they've gone
These are some thoughts of
Simple Don.

DON'S VALLEY

I found myself a valley
Where I chose to live
And decided I would take from it
No more than I could give.

It was a place of peace and harmony
Where birds sang in the trees.
I woke up every morning
And thanked the Lord for these.

For many years I lived there
At one with God's green earth
And really understood
All that life was worth.

But others came to live there
Who did not understand
And for nothing more than profit
They plundered from the land.

Now all there is barren waste
The earth is dull and dry
And as I gaze upon it
I sit here and cry.

That valley was 'The Planet Earth'
Its beauty has all died.
Mankind has destroyed it
With hate and greed and violence
And what they claimed was pride.

POOR ME

I'd like to rise like a phoenix from the ashes.
I'd like to soar like an eagle from a tree.
I'd like to leap like a lion in the jungle.
I'd like to jump like a dolphin from the sea.

But I can't, I'm only poor old me.

MONKEY TREES

I used to have lots of friends around here
But I've not seen one for many a year.
We used to live and play as we pleased
Until those men came along and cut down the trees.

They cut them all down and took them away
And without them my friends had nowhere to stay.
Those trees were our food, our life and our home
So over bare lands our familles did roam.

They wandered about all over the place
The loss of those trees was the loss of our race.
I lost my mother, my wife and my son
Shot by the tree fellers just for the fun.

Others were captured and carried away
To be put in a cage forever to stay.
It's so lonely in this land that's so bare
But I'm only a monkey, so what do you care?

It's not only me that has been treated like this
Man's polluted the rivers and killed half the fish.
Elephants also in man have no trust
They are almost extinct 'cause man wants their tusk.

There is many a rhino that could have been born
If its mother had not been slain for her horn.
I'm only a monkey, I'm furry and odd
I'm all alone and I'm saying to God:

'They have gone my Lord, they have gone.
Those beautiful, beautiful trees.
Where me and my family once used to live
Among their branches and leaves.
It has gone my Lord it has gone
The strength from my body and mind.
With my dying gasp, may I please ask
Why did you call them man kind?

MORE JOY

There was a time when Joy was mine, and life was very good.
We loved each other very much, that was always understood.

Oh! My Joy, my darling Joy
I will love you all my life
No man that ever lived, ever had a better wife.

We had some fun, we had our laughs and darling how I miss
Your loving hugs, your beaming smile and the linger of
your kiss.

There were sometimes when things were tough
And I could not face the day.
When with a smile and gentle push
You'd send me on my way.

But you had things to do elsewhere
A home to build, for us to share
So darling when you are ready don't hesitate to call
And I'll be right there by your side in God our Father's Hall.

MUGGER

There's an old fashioned lady in an old fashioned gown
Who looks so sweet as she walks around our town.
She has the smile of an angel, and the style of a queen.
She's my mother and I love her.

There's a drug-crazed mugger on the corner of the street
Who with a smile, my mother chanced to greet.
And that drug-crazed mugger, he knocked my mother down
Yeah that mugger, he killed my mother.

There's a broken-hearted widower standing by a grave
Where me and my brother are trying to be brave.
But when our father, he collapsed and died
Me and my brother, we broke down and cried.

There's a man in a grey suit sitting in a chair
They have strapped up his arms and shaved off his hair.
In just one hour that man is going to die.

He's my brother.
He shot the mugger who killed our mother.

There's a lot, a lot of people in this world of ours
Who claim that snorting coke is no worse than sniffing flowers.
I hope they have listened to this tale I had to tell
And I hope that mugger's soul will rot in Hell!

You can bury me with him now my story's told
I can't go on living and I'm only...
Nine years old.

OLD MAN

He is a timid old man, meek and mild
Who looks at life through the eyes of a child.
He has seen many years of hardship and pain
And would not like to see them again.

He has closed down his mind to the things that he fears
And it drifts back contented, to happier years.
Years when doors were open and wide
With friendship and welcoming laughter inside.

When people had little, but willingly shared
With others with less ,because that they cared.
The brothers, the sisters, the fathers and mothers
Had busy lives but cared for each other.

WHAT IS LOVE?

Rosie and Jim were sweethearts
When they were ten years old.
Rosie was coy, 'cause Jim was her boy
And this is what Rosie was told.

'I love you...I love you my darling!
And if my love you return
I will love you forever
And you can play with my...worm!

Rosie and Jim they got married
When they were both twenty four
And after the wedding was over
Jim he told Rosie the score.

' I love you...I love you my darling!
And now that you are my wife
As soon as I get my socks off
We'll have the time of our life!'

Now Rosie and Jim had been married
For nigh on forty year
When Jim he stopped huffing and puffing
And whispered in Rosie's ear.

'I love you... I love you my darling!
And I know that you love me
But we are too old for this sex lark
So get up...And make the tea!'

Now many and many years later
Both of them wrinkled and grey
Jimmy he turned to his Rosie
And here's what he had to say.

'I love you...I love you my darling!
My darling I love you so!
And if you can't get up the stairs dear
Then you can...borrow my POE!'
          That's love!

POLICE CHASE

The policeman he did chase me
He chased me on his bike.
He's not the sort of copper
Anyone could like.

I knew if he could catch me
He would clip me around the ear
All because I put a slug
In his pint of beer.

I hid behind a tree
And as his bike whizzed clear (past)
I took out my catapult
And shot him up the rear (arse).

I caught him plum dead centre
He let out a mighty roar
And rode in to the village shop
And straight out the back door.

'Get out my way!' The copper yelled
As six customers he felled.

A woman that was in there
Practising the Piana
Yelled 'I'm reporting you
I do not like your manner.'

A granny with a pram did amble
And out the way she had to scramble

As she heard the copper cry
'Get out my way!' as he whizzed by.
That old copper, that old Bill
On his bike whizzed down a hill.
A rock at the bottom, the bike did stop
It stopped the bike but not the cop.

In his uniform of blue
Through the air the copper flew
As his helmet hit the ground
It made a funny scratching sound.

It didn't stop until the spike
Went straight through a water pipe.
Water shot out in a jet
And made the postman soaking wet.

As the bedraggled copper rose
The postman hit him on the nose.
'What's your game?' The cop did cry
Then punched the postman in the eye.

'I know my rights!' the postman said
And hit the copper on the head.
The policeman yelled, ' You can't do that!'
And whacked the postman with his hat.

'What's going on?' The Baker yelled
And by the other two were felled.
'I saw it all,' the old Granny croaked
'It was all your fault that he got soaked.'

The baker sprawling on the ground
By chance the copper's helmet found
As he pulled it out the pipe
Water shot it out of sight.

'That's my hat!' The copper roared.
In granny's ear, and she was floored.

From the pipe the water flowed
And made a river of the road.
The baker said, 'I will go
And get a plumber to stop the flow.'

'Oh dear! Oh dear,' the plumber said
As he frowned and scratched his head
'Pipes in the road I cannot mend
For the water board you must send.

The baker spoke to the water board bloke
Who thought it was a tremendous joke.
'I know you are all wet and muddied
But we can't get through, the road is flooded!'

It was then the plumber the suggestion made
Why not send for the Fire Brigade.

Like newborn lambs to the slaughter
The firemen drove through the water.
They did not know as they set their pump
That the copper had the hump.

From the day's events, the cop was smarting
And as the pumping they were starting
He booked the fire brigade
For parking!

As the fire chief gave the cop a thump
Poor old Gran got sucked up the pump.

Stuck half way up the spout

It took ten men to pull her out
'Oh where,' she said, 'is my Sam
I left him laying in his pram.'

Out of the pram floating down the street
Were a pair of enormous feet.
That baby Sam he was a whopper
When he grows up he' ll be a copper.

'Save him! Save him!' Gran did scream
As Sam went floating down the stream.
'They will do their best,' the fire chief mouthed
'If I could swim I go myself.'

The cop recovering from the blow
Said 'You stay here, and I will go
And don't you move for flood or fire
Until I get back with a Black Myria.'

'By you lot I won't be bested
When I get back you will be arrested.'

'When the fire chief asked, 'What for?'
The cop yelled 'Laying down the law!'

All this time the postman chose to linger
And block the bust pipe with his finger.
But his effort was in vain
The road was like the River Seine.

As the copper he did hasten
On his bike to the station
That copper he spotted I
So up the road I had to fly.

I ran straight into the pram

It tipped up and out flew Sam.
Through the air young Sam soared
'Catch him! Catch him!' Granny roared.

'What's going on?' the baker asked
As the empty pram whizzed past.
The postman caught the little chappy
Who'd done a dollop in his nappy.

'Take him! Take him!' The postman did yell
As he staggered from the smell.
'Give him here,' old Gran did shout
Then smelt the dollop and passed out.

When the empty pram was seen
Floating slowly down the stream.
Sam's mother yelled, 'What have they done
With my poor Sam, my darling Son?'
'It's all your fault!' Old gran did yell
As she recovered from the smell.
And at my head she did wallop
With a nappy full of dollop.

The plumber, he repaired the pipe
The copper at my ear did swipe.
His mother and the baker man
Took Sam home in his pram.

The fire brigade full of elation
Returned in triumph to their station.
And in reflecting, I was a mug
In the copper's beer to put a slug.